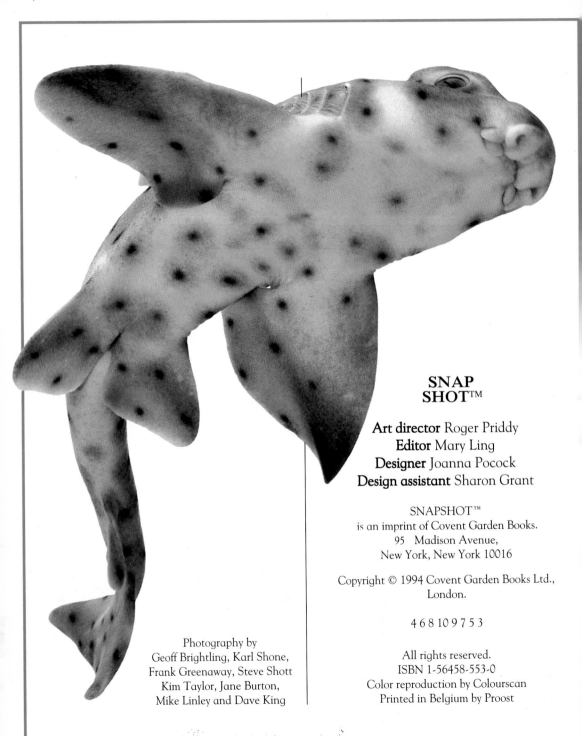

SNAP SHOT™

Art director Roger Priddy
Editor Mary Ling
Designer Joanna Pocock
Design assistant Sharon Grant

SNAPSHOT™
is an imprint of Covent Garden Books.
95 Madison Avenue,
New York, New York 10016

4 6 8 10 9 7 5 3

ISBN 1-56458-553-0
Color reproduction by Colourscan
Printed in Belgium by Proost

Photography by
Geoff Brightling, Karl Shone,
Frank Greenaway, Steve Shott
Kim Taylor, Jane Burton,
Mike Linley and Dave King

European fire salamander

Color me mad!

Chameleons are amazing little lizards. They cc
change color at will to hide from enemies, sned
up on dinner, or let other chameleons know
exactly how they feel. If you annoy one, it may
turn black with anger!

Horny beast
Jackson's chameleon has three horns on its
head. They are used to fight other males
when looking
for a mate.

Rainbow colors

Look out for the tongue
it's as long as the body!

Neat feet
A chameleon's
feet grab onto
branches like pliers.
It can also loop its tail
around a branch to hold on.

A tail like a lasso

Pick a color, any color!

Torro!
Though it can wave its triple horns and look fierce, this Jackson's chameleon is only 12 in (30cm) long.

Horns

Eyes that swivel

Two at a time
Each eye can move on its own, so a chameleon can look two ways at the same time.

Ready, aim, splat!
A chameleon keeps its tongue coiled up in its mouth. When an insect comes close, it takes aim and shoots its tongue out like a bullet. A sticky pad at the end traps the bug and reels it in.

Feet for gripping branches

Chameleon

Smooth and bumpy

Telling frogs and toads apart is
a tricky business. Usually
frogs are smooth-
skinned, have webbed
feet, and stay close to
water. Toads have
rough, warty
skin and live
on land.

At home in the trees

Smoot
skin lik
a fro

Asian tree toad

**Three-toed
tree toad**
Most people
confuse this Asian
tree toad with a
frog. Its skin is fairly
smooth and it has big
gripping pads on its
fingertips, just like
tree frogs

Leapfrog
Frogs hunt flies, crickets, and other fast-moving insects. They can leap with split-second timing to snap up any insect that lands nearby.

Look at those super long legs!

Frog

Legs at full stretch

Leafy horns help toads hide

...dy that ...eezes flat

...sian leaf toad

Horns for hiding
This little toad has horns above its eyes that look like leaves. They help it blend in with its home, the forest floor.

Why does a toad have horns?

Leaping lizard

High in the branches of a tree in the jungle, a little lizard spies a hungry hawk. In panic, it leaps. It sails through the air and lands on a nearby tree. The flying gecko lives to see another day!

Gecko

Meet Mr. Super Glue!

Sticky fingers

A gecko grips so strongly, it can run upside-down along a branch, or cling so tightly to a window it can't be pulled off without cracking the glass. The secret is the scales under each toe: they are covered with thousands of tiny hairs that stick like glue.

Toes with sharp claws cling to trees.

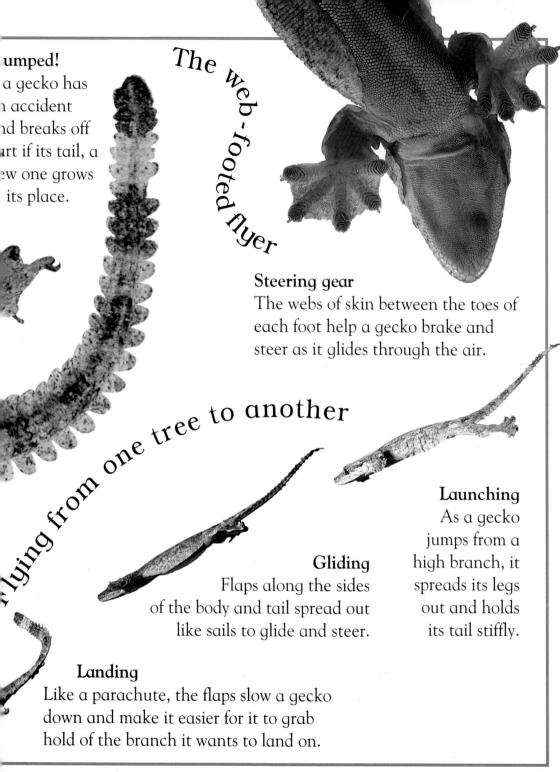

umped!
a gecko has
n accident
d breaks off
rt if its tail, a
w one grows
its place.

The web-footed flyer

Steering gear
The webs of skin between the toes of
each foot help a gecko brake and
steer as it glides through the air.

flying from one tree to another

Launching
As a gecko
jumps from a
high branch, it
spreads its legs
out and holds
its tail stiffly.

Gliding
Flaps along the sides
of the body and tail spread out
like sails to glide and steer.

Landing
Like a parachute, the flaps slow a gecko
down and make it easier for it to grab
hold of the branch it wants to land on.

11

Night flyer

The fruit bat can fly like a dream. Like all bats, its wings are sheets of skin stretched over the arms and long finger bones.

Hanging ten
Bats hang upside down by their ten toes even when they are fast asleep.

How blind is a bat?
Bats can see perfectly well. But since they hunt for flying insects at night, they rely on their terrific sense of hearing to track down their food.

Ears pick up the echo

What big ears you have!

How do fruit bats hunt?
They depend on good eyesight, and a great sense of smell to home in on plump figs, juicy mangoes, and ripe bananas.

Daubenton bat

Bat arms have elbows

Neither meat-eater nor vegetable-eater!

Fancy some juice?

Fruit bats fly slowly, searching out ripe fruit in the forest. They don't eat the whole fruit. They simply bite into it with their sharp teeth and suck out the sweet juices.

Fruit bat

Flapping wings are almost silent

Look at you, all skin and bones!

Sounds like supper

An insect-eating bat uses a high-pitched sound like radar to track down prey. The echos steer the bat toward its target, even in complete darkness.

Bat wings

Bats are the only mammals that can fly. Their wings are strong, but very light, just like the wings of a small plane. Bat wings have no feathers.

Breaking out

Just because an animal lays eggs doesn't mean it's a bird. Insects, fish, and reptiles all lay eggs too. Snakes, like most reptiles, care for themselves after hatching, just like little grown-ups.

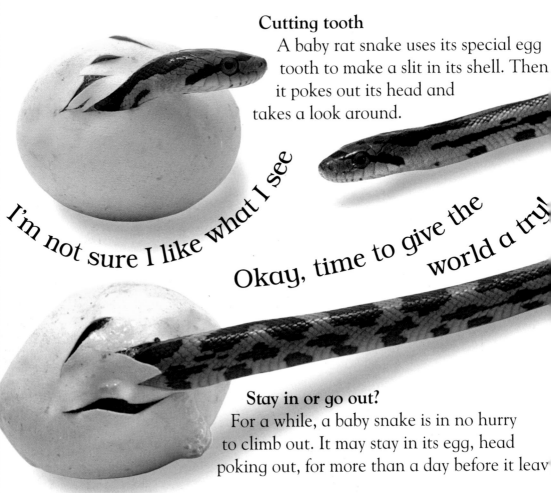

Cutting tooth
A baby rat snake uses its special egg tooth to make a slit in its shell. Then it pokes out its head and takes a look around.

I'm not sure I like what I see

Okay, time to give the world a try!

Stay in or go out?
For a while, a baby snake is in no hurry to climb out. It may stay in its egg, head poking out, for more than a day before it leav

Time to see the world
The young snake begins to slide out of its shell. It is completely alone. It doesn't need parents to feed or care for it. It is independent.

Look, no parents!

Small ear slits are behind the head

A lot in a little
Finally, the snake emerges from its shell. A baby snake may be seven times longer than the egg from which it is born!

If I don't like it, can I climb back in?

Rat snake

Slither!

Never play with a snake. Each year, about 30,000 people die from being bitten by snakes!

Hognose snake

It's *as* long as *a* person is ta*ll*

Old flat nos*e*

The 60 in (150 cm*)* hognose snake i*s* relatively harmless*,* preferring t*o* hiss loudly, o*r* even play dea*d* when disturbed*.*

King of the snakes

A king snake is one that hunts other snakes. This Californian king snake eats lizards and small snakes.

Seen any yummy snakes around?

The tongue can tell if prey is nearby

King snake

Bat snack!

The red-tailed racer prowls around the entrance to caves and grabs bats that flutter c*out* at night. A single bat is enough food for days.

Do you think I look like corn?

Corn-fused
The corn snake isn't poisonous and it doesn't eat corn!

Corn snake

Belly-up
Its name comes from marks on its belly, which look like Indian corn.

I'm a bat-catcher!

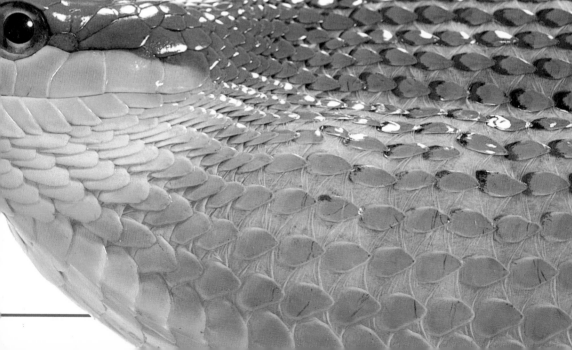

Water and land

Salamanders are born in water, but live on land. Many have no lungs. Instead, they breathe through their skin and throat.

Marbled newt

Wet fire

The fire salamander of Europe is a stubby little animal, usually no more than 12 in (30 cm) long. It lives close to water and hunts slow-moving prey, such as earthworms.

Hides under rocks and logs · or in damp earth

Its damp skin helps it breathe.

Fire salamander

Meet the newt

The newt is a cousin of the salamander and has the same long tail and soft, moist body.

This newt comes from France and Spain

Part-time hunters!

Newts and salamanders hunt worms, snails, and insects. But they spend most of their time resting.

Moist, slimy, and poisonous

Tasty treat?

These salamanders have special glands filled with poison in their skin.

Tree salamanders

Steer clear

The yellow marks on their backs warn off other animals.

19

Armored animals

For tortoises on land and turtles in the water, safety depends on having an extra-strong shell. When there's danger around, they hide inside.

Alligator turtle

Snap! Ouch!!
The alligator snapper can chomp most things with its bladelike jaws – fish, crabs, turtles – even human hands and feet!

Powerful legs have claws to grip and hold prey

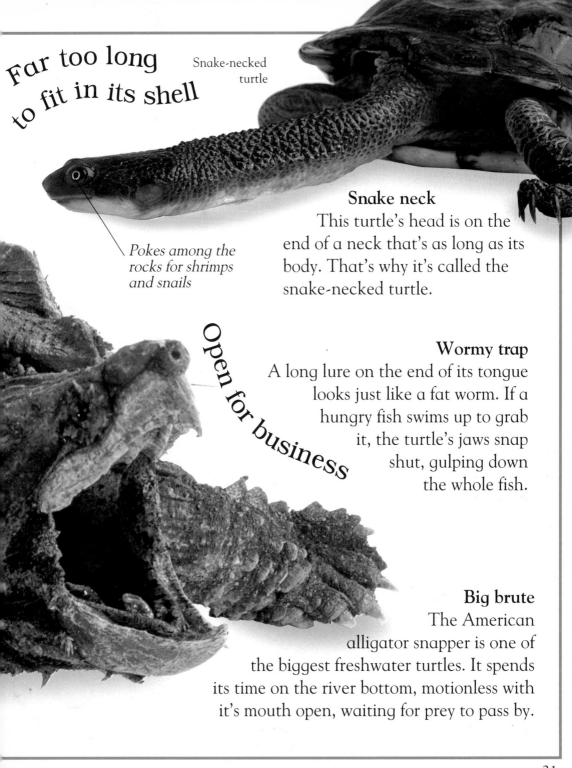

Far too long to fit in its shell

Snake-necked turtle

Pokes among the rocks for shrimps and snails

Snake neck
This turtle's head is on the end of a neck that's as long as its body. That's why it's called the snake-necked turtle.

Open for business

Wormy trap
A long lure on the end of its tongue looks just like a fat worm. If a hungry fish swims up to grab it, the turtle's jaws snap shut, gulping down the whole fish.

Big brute
The American alligator snapper is one of the biggest freshwater turtles. It spends its time on the river bottom, motionless with it's mouth open, waiting for prey to pass by.

Living in a shell

A crab lives inside a thick case of shell that protects almost all of its body. Crabs have four pairs of legs for walking and running, and another pair with strong pincer claws for feeding.

Here comes the hard par

See here
Most crabs have eyes that bulge out of the shell. A few have eyes on the ends of stalks, so they can lie under the sand and still see.

Nip and tuck
This crab has a huge pair of pincers that can deliver a very painful nip.

Always walk sideways so your legs don't tangle

The mouth is tucked underneath the front edge of the shell

Giant pincers for grabbing and tearing up food

Household fly trap

If you lived in the tropics and had a little lizard in your house, you would think yourself lucky. Lizards run up and down walls, gobbling tasty bugs.

Gecko

Barking mad
Geckos can make an incredible noise by clicking their tongues. Some bark like dogs. Others chirp like crickets.

Toe pads help grip

A natural acrobat

Day job
Most geckos are awake at night, but the Madagascar day gecko is up with human beings. It eats insects and fruit, and sips nectar from flowers.

Just like mom, only smaller

Long tail for
balancing

Mom doesn't care

A mother gecko lays eggs on trees or in
rocks. Then she leaves
her young as soon
as they hatch.

Thick scaly skin, like a suit of armor

Iguana

Nostrils
for smelling

Long pointed scales

Skin care

In South America, the most com-
mon lizard is the iguana. There are
hundreds of different kinds. Often
their skin is covered with spikes,
crests, frills, and horns. This is for
protection, and to show off to others.

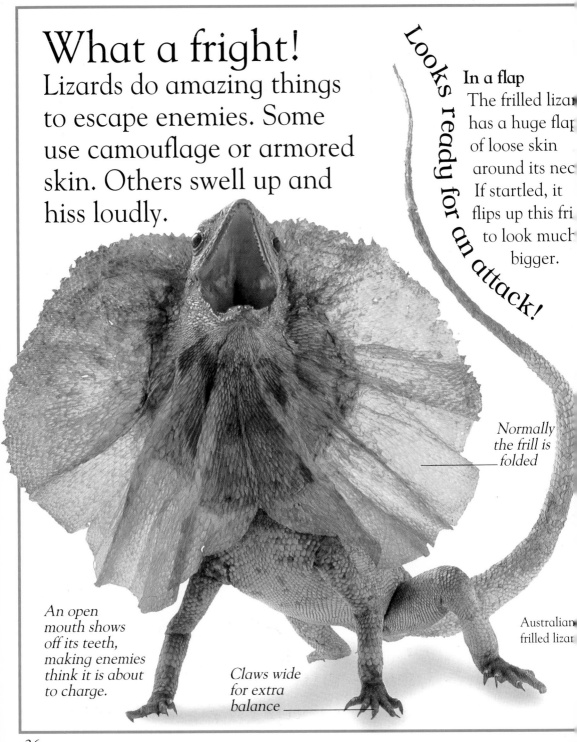

What a fright!

Lizards do amazing things to escape enemies. Some use camouflage or armored skin. Others swell up and hiss loudly.

In a flap
The frilled lizard has a huge flap of loose skin around its neck. If startled, it flips up this frill to look much bigger.

Normally the frill is folded

An open mouth shows off its teeth, making enemies think it is about to charge.

Claws wide for extra balance

Australian frilled lizard

26

Grow another

This little lizard had a close brush with death, but escaped by shedding part of its tail. Better the tail than a life! Soon a new tail grows back.

Tail recently broken off

New tail – after two months

Another day, another tail

Ready to leap up and run

After eight months the tail is complete

On your mark ...

Despite its name, the crested water dragon spends most of its time in the trees. When danger threatens, it rears up on its strong hind legs.

Get set ...

The wary lizard looks around, preparing to run for its life.

Go!

The lizard's back legs are much stronger than its front ones, and quickly power it along.

Water dragon lizard

Monsters of the deep

Many of the strangest-looking animals live in the sea. Some are gigantic, others are tiny, but all look like nightmarish creatures.

Bullhead shark

Never both
with hum
—bei

Broken nose

The bullhead shark looks as if somebody has given it a nasty punch on the nose. But this flat shape is exactly right for rooting about on the ocean floor.

*Twists and bunches ...
just like a ribbon*

Ribbon eel

Tied up in kno

The ribbon eel has a incredibly long boo that looks like it cou tie itself in knots.

with t

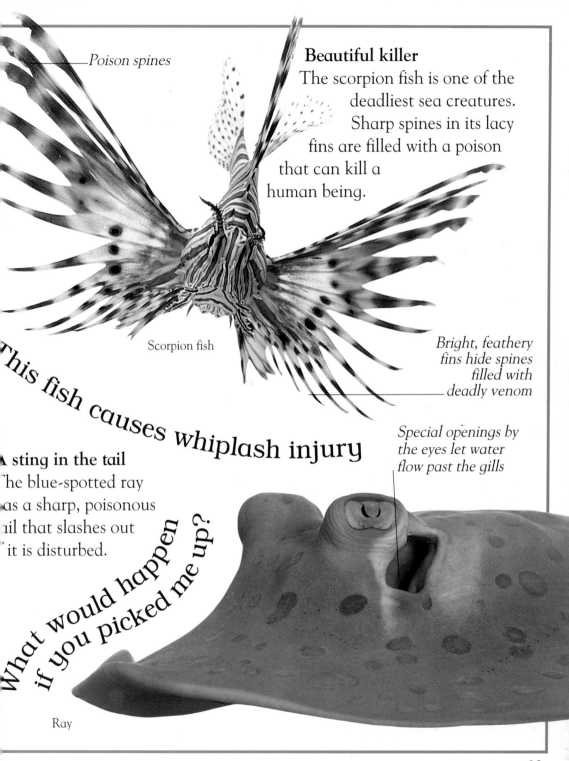

Poison spines

Beautiful killer

The scorpion fish is one of the deadliest sea creatures. Sharp spines in its lacy fins are filled with a poison that can kill a human being.

Scorpion fish

Bright, feathery fins hide spines filled with deadly venom

This fish causes whiplash injury

A sting in the tail

The blue-spotted ray has a sharp, poisonous tail that slashes out if it is disturbed.

Special openings by the eyes let water flow past the gills

What would happen if you picked me up?

Ray

Index

Five fiendish questions

1) What animal turns black when it is angry

2) What lizard starts to fly after it leaps?

3) Which creature sleeps upside down?

4) How many people are killed by snakes every year?

(a) more than 30
(b) more than 300
(c) more than 3,000
(d) more than 30,000
(e) none

5) Which turtle is like an alligator?

Answers on page 32

How will this reptile catch its next meal?

Answer on next page

31

Answers

From page 30:
1. The chameleon
2. The flying gecko
3. The bat
4. More than 30,000
5. The alligator snapper

From page 31:
It will sit patiently until an insect comes near, then open its mouth and zap it with a sticky tongue that's as long as its body. It has deadly accurate aim.